God is With You

JOHN QUINLAN

VERITAS

Published 1986 by
Veritas Publications
7-8 Lower Abbey Street
Dublin 1

ISBN 0 86217 252 7

Nihil obstat
Mgr Michael O'Flaherty
Censor Deputatus

Imprimatur
✠ Diarmaid Ó Súilleabháin
Bishop of Kerry

The author and publishers are grateful to the following for permission to quote from their copyright material: Darton, Longman and Todd Ltd and Doubleday & Co. Inc. for extracts from *The Jerusalem Bible*, published and copyright 1966, 1967 and 1968; McCrimmon Publishing Co. Ltd, 10-12 High Street, Great Wakering, Essex, for extracts from *Prayers for the Sick* by Michael Hollings and Etta Gullick; Thomas O'Keeffe for 'Prayer when Suffering', 'Feeling Better', 'I find it difficult to accept this illness', prayers for a safe delivery, thanksgiving after delivery, dedication of a child to Mary, Prayer of Parents, Prayer of a mother who has lost her baby, Prayers of an Unmarried Mother.
The author also wishes to thank Most Rev. Diarmaid Ó Súilleabháin, Bishop of Kerry; Rev. Thomas O'Keeffe; Rt Rev. Mgr Michael O'Flaherty; V. Rev. Patrick McCarthy PP; the late Mgr JJ Murphy and all the patients and staff with whom he has worked for their assistance, advice and encouragement.

Cover design: Eddie McManus
Typesetting: Printset & Design Ltd
Printed in the Republic of Ireland by Mount Salus Press Ltd

To Mam and Dad
(RIP)

Contents

Foreword

Although he is still a young man, Father John Quinlan has many years' experience as a Hospital Chaplain.

He is familiar with every detail of hospital life and routine, but, what is more important, he is deeply sensitive to the hopes and fears of the many patients who are committed to his care.

For many of these patients, particularly those who are elderly, merely being away from home is an unfamiliar and upsetting experience. Add to this the worry arising from their illness, and it becomes obvious that they are very much in need of help and reassurance. Idle and sentimental catch-phrases are of no use whatever.

This little book is designed, from start to finish, to help those who are undergoing this ordeal of separation from home, and the worries and fears associated with 'being ill'.

The author rightly is at pains to show the true place of suffering in the Christian context. The sufferings of Christ were the means of our Redemption, and God has used suffering and self-denial as the means of sanctification and purification in the lives of his specially chosen ones — the Saints of the Church.

This disposes of the pernicious error that suffering is to be seen as a sign of God's displeasure, or as a punishment for sin. Anyone who reads and ponders over this booklet will never again be tempted to ask: "Why did God do this to me?" He will be more disposed to say: "God's Will be done".

The book contains a wonderful collection of prayers and meditations. They are suitably short and simple, easily said, and never wearying.

While the book is primarily intended for the sick, it can be used with great profit by anybody and everybody.

I gladly recommend it, and I pray that God may bless its author, and also bestow consolation and health on all who use it.

✠ Diarmaid
Bishop of Kerry

Message of Pope John XXIII to the Sick

Cheer up, **God is with you.**
You suffer, it is true;
but **He** is near you.
Trust in **Him,** as you would trust in your own
Father.
If **He** has let you suffer,
it is because **He** sees something good in it
which today you do not yet know.
Your peace of mind is in your **"Trust in God"**
Who can never let you down.

". . . The immense fruitfulness of
suffering . . ."

The Passion of Christ will reveal to you the
immense fruitfulness of suffering in the
sanctification of souls and the salvation of the
world . . . Here in your illness is the instrument
offered to you by Providence so that you can fill
up those things that are wanting in the sufferings
of Christ . . . for his body which is the Church.

Pope John XXIII

Life in Hospital

Being in hospital makes one anxious. You are in
a strange world — so different from your home.
You may feel lonely and troubled that your
world is falling apart. You are cut off from your

family, job, neighbours, friends and from the normal flow of life. You wonder how the others are getting on without you. You may feel weak or afraid — afraid of death, afraid of the unknown or afraid that you won't be understood. How can one who has never suffered arthritis know the pain of someone who can hardly move from a chair? How can someone who can hear clearly sense the pain of a person who doesn't hear even when they shout and get cross at him? You may be impatient waiting for various tests or for an operation. You may feel that your recovery is slow and you wonder how long more this will go on.

In whatever situation you find yourself, you need support.

Remember that in this hospital you are among friends. We know that it can never be like home but there is a happy atmosphere here. Every member of the staff has one aim — to help you and your relatives while you are here and to send you home safe and sound. You might spare a thought for them in your prayers and offer a word of appreciation now and then.

Remember too that **God is with you** here. It is difficult to pray while you are sick. You have plenty of time, yet you don't seem to be able to pray. God understands this and He won't fail you. You may feel at times that He has abandoned you, but He is very much with you in your sickness.

Here we suggest some prayers for you in hospital. Don't try to read this book from cover to cover. Pick the prayer that suits you and say it slowly. God will help and comfort you through these prayers.

§ § §

Jesus said: **"Know that I am with you always;** yes, to the end of time". *(Mt 28:20)*

One Day at a Time

A woman who had a serious accident had to have a painful operation and was in bed for a long time. One day she asked her doctor "how long will I have to lie here and be helpless?" "Only one day at a time", he answered.

She felt much better then and very often during her long stay in hospital the words came back to encourage her: "only one day at a time".

If you think in terms of weeks, time seems very long. But if you take one day at a time and offer it to God, it might not be so bad.

Footprints

One night a man had a dream.
He dreamed he was walking along
the beach with the LORD. Across
the sky flashed scenes from his
life. For each scene, he noticed
two sets of footprints in the sand
. . . one belonging to him and the
other to the LORD.

When the last scene of his life
flashed before him, he looked back
at the footprints in the sand. He noticed that
many times along the path of his life there was
only one set of footprints. He also noticed that
this
HAPPENED AT THE VERY LOWEST AND
SADDEST TIMES IN HIS LIFE.

This really bothered him and he questioned the LORD about it.

"Lord, you said that once I decided to follow you, you'd walk with me all the way. But I have noticed that during the most troublesome times in my life, there is only one set of footprints. I don't understand why, when I needed You most, You would leave me".

The LORD replied: "My precious, precious child, I love you and I would never leave you during your times of trial and suffering. When you see only one set of footprints, it was then that I carried you".

Author unknown

The Mystery of Sickness

Sickness and pain have always been a burden to us and have puzzled our understanding. When we meet sickness and pain we are faced with a mystery we don't fully understand in this life. They bring home to us what things are really important in life, as things we thought were important don't seem to matter any more.

Christians suffer sickness and pain as do all others. Our faith won't do away with sickness but it will help us to bear it bravely and to fight against it and eventually, if necessary, to accept it.

Suffering in itself has no value. You may feel that it removes all meaning from life. It can make you feel that you neither matter nor are needed. It calls for practical response. It is important to know that sickness and pain are not a punishment for sin. Consider the following passage from St. John's Gospel:

The Cure of the man born blind
"As Jesus went along, he saw a man who had been blind from birth. His disciples asked him, 'Rabbi, who sinned, this man or his parents, for him to have been born blind?' 'Neither he nor his parents sinned' Jesus answered, 'he was born blind so that the works of God might be displayed in him'.

Having said this, He spat on the ground, made a paste with the spittle, put this over the eyes of the blind man, and said to him, 'Go and wash in the pool of Siloam (a name that means sent)'. So the blind man went off and washed himself and came away with his sight restored''.

(Jn 9:1-3, 5-7)

Sickness, suffering and death are part of life and we should fight them with all our strength, as Christ did. Only as a last resort did He accept them and offer them for the Redemption of the world. He recognised the mystery and only then did he accept death.

''The sufferings of Christ were the means of our Redemption, and God has used suffering and self-denial as the means of sanctification and purification in the lives of his specially chosen ones — the Saints of the Church.'' For some, serious sickness and the strangeness of the hospital threatens the meaning and value of their religious life. For others the experience of sickness can enrich them in ways never experienced before. It evokes a deep appreciation of God and they feel very close to Christ. For many, sickness is an experience which brings them face to face with themselves. They have time to question and to think about what really matters in life. It is a turning point in many lives. In a sense, despite all those around you, when you are sick you are left very much alone to come to terms with yourself and with God. But **God is with you.** As the Israelites of old used to say, God is by the bedside of the sick.

You also have with you those who love you and pray for you, other sick people and in fact the whole Church. Sickness calls on you to abandon yourself to God even though you cannot fully understand His ways. You must try to trust God and accept your own powerlessness. Abandoning yourself to faith in God is your victory.

The Sacrament of the Anointing of the Sick

One of the main concerns of Christ's life was his care and concern for the sick. As someone put it: "Every time you meet Jesus in the Gospels, He is either actually healing someone, or has just come from healing someone, or is on His way to it". He stretched out His hand to give sight to the blind, hearing to the deaf, to lift up the cripple and heal the leper. Jesus knew the reality of sickness. He saw what it did to people and He knew how sick people felt. He knew the anxiety they felt. He knew that they sometimes felt angry and guilty; that they worried and doubted. He knew that they often felt lonely. He healed the cripple who said to him "Sir I have no one". *(Jn 5:7)* He knew that they found it difficult to pray, to resist temptation and to trust in God. He always healed these troubled feelings of theirs. He accepted sickness as part of life and fought against it.

The Sacrament of the Anointing of the Sick is one of the ways Jesus continues his care and concern for sick people. He asked his followers to show this same care and concern. This sacrament is a special meeting with Christ for the sick person. It is the outward sign which makes you aware that **God is with you.**

The form of the sacrament is the **laying-on-of-hands in silence** and **anointing with oil.** Jesus laid his hands on the sick to heal them and

11

comfort them. **Laying-on-of-hands** in silence is a sign of the Presence of God. **Anointing with oil** is a sign of healing. As he anoints with oil on the forehead and on the palms of the hands, the priest says:

"Through this holy anointing may the Lord in his love and mercy help you with the grace of the Holy Spirit." Amen.

"May the Lord who frees you from sin save you and raise you up." Amen.

These and the prayer of faith are the visible signs that **God is with you.**

This sacrament eases your anxiety. It gives you strength to resist the temptation to despair and to give up prayer. It strengthens your faith and encourages your trust in God. If necessary, it forgives your sins. It brings you that comfort and peace which Christ alone can give. You can then bear your sufferings bravely and fight against them.

Like all sacraments, this Sacrament of the Anointing of the Sick must be received with **faith** — faith enough to believe that the same Jesus who brought healing and forgiveness two thousand years ago is with you; faith enough to keep trusting in God at a time when your faith is tested by a sickness that seems wasteful and pointless. For the person with faith, meeting Jesus in the Sacrament of the Sick is as real as his own meetings with the sick while he was on earth.

At one time this sacrament was too closely associated with death. Jesus never meant this to happen. St James says that the sick should send for the priest to pray with them and anoint them with oil.

"If one of you is sick, he should send for the elders of the church, and they must anoint him with oil in the name of the Lord and pray over him. The prayer of faith will save the sick man and the Lord will raise him up again; and if he has committed any sins, he will be forgiven.

(James 5:13-15)

The Second Vatican Council tells us to forget old ideas about the anointing of the sick and accept it as the healing gift described by St James.

St Mark, in his Gospel, tells us that "the disciples anointed many sick people with oil and cured them."

(Mk 6:13)

This sacrament should be associated with healing and trust in God. To receive it is to face the challenge of sickness. It helps you to cope with your sickness. It reminds you of God at a time when you may be finding it difficult to pray because of your sickness. Above all, it reassures you that **God is with you.**

If the Sacrament of the Anointing of the Sick is offered to you, welcome it. If you would like to receive it, ask the priest.

Prayers to be Said by a Sick Person

Prayers after being admitted to hospital

Lord, I do not want to be here. I am not used to this kind of place. I find it strange. I feel lonely and awkward here. There is no privacy but people continually around, bustling and noisy. I will never have any peace and quiet in which to pray to you. For even in the night, people call out and nurses rush around. Lord, give me a sense of Your Presence deep inside me; give me a sense of peace that will persist under all the fuss and noise. Amen.

§ § §

In this ward, Jesus, there are many who are suffering. Some maybe are dying. Some must feel very alone in their pain. Help us to bear our crosses of worry, sickness and loss of faith, so that we can help those who do not know you. Amen.

§ § §

Lord, I believe in you. Increase my faith and trust. Heal me not only in body but in mind and soul as well so that I can be the kind of person you want me to be. Amen.

Suffering and the Risen Christ

Risen Lord, I thank you for being with me.

Help me always to remember that you have conquered pain, suffering and death. You suffered and then found joy. I unite my pain with the pain you suffered so that I too may find joy and be filled with the glory which you have won. Amen.

Prayer with suffering
Lord Jesus, I think of the pains you endured for me; the great sadness of the garden, your scourging and crowning, your cross, your death. You had to suffer to enter into your glory. The sufferings of this time are not to be compared with the glory that is to come. In the strength of your Spirit, I join my sufferings to yours for the redemption of the world. Amen.

Prayer before an operation
Jesus, I am very afraid. I do not know what is going to happen to me. I have absolutely no control over what happens and I dislike not being in control. I am afraid of the loss of consciousness that the anaesthetic will bring. I worry that I will be a burden to others after the operation and that I will not be active again. Lord, help me to trust you. Help me to remember that at this moment I have a great deal to be thankful for. I am grateful for the skill and kindness of the doctors and nurses. Help me to be calm and relaxed. Remove my fear and that of my relatives. Let my prayer be the prayer of Jesus himself; "Father, into your hands I commit my spirit". Give me the faith to

realise that nothing can separate me from your
love in Christ Jesus our Lord. Amen.

Why did this happen to me?
Lord, why do I have to be sick like this? Why
do I have to endure pain? I just don't
understand it. I have lived a good honest life
and now this! Why me? I can't understand why
you do this sort of thing to the people who try
to follow you and keep your commandments.
It's not much consolation either to think of what
happened to Jesus. Can't you explain your ways
a little, for they seem unfair to me, Lord?

Give me the strength to bear whatever happens
to me, however puzzled I may be. Do not leave
me now. Amen.

Feeling bitter?
O God, it is better to speak to you frankly about
things than to bottle them up. I cannot help
wondering why this should have happened to
me. I cannot help feeling bitter and resentful. I
know that I shouldn't feel this way. People
annoy me when they tell me it is all for the best.
Lord, I know that there just isn't any answer, at
least not just now. So, help me to accept what I
can't understand. Keep me from self-pity.
Amen.

Feeling lonely?
Jesus, I know that you are with me now because
you have told me that you are with me always.

16

Yes, Lord, I feel lonely. You know what it is like to be alone at the time of greatest need. So please Lord, give me what you had — a few friends to support and accept me. Amen.

I find it hard to accept this sickness
Father, I find it hard to accept this sickness. I am impatient. I find it hard to speak to anyone. I find it hard to talk to you. I am wrapped up in pity and worry for myself. I worry about the things I would like to do but now I cannot. At a time like this I find it hard to believe in you, to trust, to love. I know you really care for me. I cast all my troubles upon you. I leave myself entirely in your kind hands. Not my will but yours be done. Amen.

Depressed?
Lord, when this depression comes on me I am weighed down. All joy leaves me and I am in a state of sadness that seems unending. There seems to be no way out. Lord, do not let this come upon me again. If it does, let me know that you are in it with me. Make me realise that you shared this sort of depression on the cross and that you understand the awfulness from which one cannot escape. Amen.

§   §   §

Lord, I am full of sadness and I cannot get over it. I suppose I don't even want to, yet I am miserable beyond belief and remaining in it is hell. How can you leave me like this, Lord? I cry out to you for help. Give me some glimpse of hope. Help me, for I cannot help myself. Amen.

Prayer in time of mental anguish
God, sometimes I think physical pain is less hard to bear than mental suffering. A toothache or a broken leg is at least in one place. But anxiety or tension, guilt or indecision is everywhere at once — and nowhere. When Jesus said, ''Not my will but yours be done'', did His pain go away? I don't think so. But I do believe that You made it possible for Him to bear it. Do for me, Father, whatever it was You did for Him. As I try to imitate His fidelity to Your will may I experience Your peace — the peace that, somehow, can exist in the midst of great suffering. Amen.

In Pain
Lord, have mercy! What more can I say with this intolerable pain which grips me? I cannot bear it. Was it like this on the Cross?

I offer it for all mankind and particularly for those dear to me whose needs I know. I cannot think or act as I would, but let the bearing of this pain be my prayer. It cannot go on for ever, for either it will get worse and kill me, or there will come relief. Lord, thy will be done. Whatever it may be — Lord, have mercy. Amen.

Worried

When you're troubled and worried
And sick at heart
And your plans are upset
And your world falls apart;
Remember God's ready
And waiting to share
The burden you find
Much too heavy to bear.
So with faith "let go"
And let God lead the way
Into a brighter
And less troubled day.
For God has a plan for everyone
If we learn to pray
"Thy will be done".
For nothing in life
Is without God's design
For each life is fashioned
By the Hand that's Divine.

Afraid of death

Lord, you did not seem to want to die — at least
not that way. You did ask your Father "let this
chalice pass" — but he didn't and I can see
why. But this chalice, my sickness which they
won't tell me is dying, but which I half know
and half dread — if only, if only. There is so
much I still want to do, Lord, and I'm afraid.
Help me to be calm and help me say 'not my
will but Yours be done'. Amen.

§   §   §

"Do not be afraid, for I have redeemed you; I have called you by your name. You are mine . . . **I will be with you;** . . . For I am your God, your saviour.
Because you are precious in my eyes, I love you. Do not be afraid for **I am with you**". *(Is 43)*

A prayer about death
Father, I don't want to die. I don't even like to think about it. But death is inevitable. And every death, near or far, reminds me of my own. Will it be the end of everything I know? The final separation from those I love? The total interruption of works that are important to me? What I can't seem to get into my head is that death is part of life. Otherwise You wouldn't let it happen to Your Son — or to me. Give me, please, a new kind of vision, a fresh burst of energy to let myself go when the time comes. Help me to see the end as a beginning, the parting as a reunion, the last curtain as the lifting of a veil. Amen.

Finding it difficult to pray
Lord, now I am ill, I have plenty of time to pray, but I am too taken up with my pain and fears to do more than say, please help me to endure, don't leave me, and remember me when I become so concerned with myself that I forget you. Help me to put myself in your hands even though all I want to do is complain and resent the suffering. Never let your spirit cease to pray in the depth of my being, I beg you. Amen.

Complaining
Lord, I am sick, in pain, drugged. I want to
accept this sickness and yet when anyone visits
me I am tempted to complain endlessly about
what is happening to me. Lord, help me to
overcome this and to be alert to the troubles and
sufferings of others as well. Amen.

Sleepless
Lord, I can't go to sleep and there is nothing I
want more. I want to forget my difficulties for a
while. I think of Your sleepless night in
Gethsemane and with You I say, "Father, not
my will but Yours be done". Help me to pray
for all those who lie awake tonight. Amen.

Waiting
Lord, I am anxiously waiting (for this
operation/for the results of x-rays, tests/for the
doctor). Stop me from feeling frustrated and
help me to use this time to pray for others and
for myself. Help me to realise that no time spent
waiting with you is wasted. Amen.

I brought this sickness on myself
Lord, I know I brought this sickness on myself.
But I was so depressed, Lord, that I just
couldn't stand it any longer. I know that you
understand. Please forgive me and help me back
again. Amen.

It takes so long to get better
O God, I'm all right so long as I am lying here

in bed, or so long as I don't try to do anything; but I have just no strength. I can't hurry; I can't even do anything quickly; I have to take my time — and it is a long time. It is so discouraging to feel weak and to feel tired. I want to get back to work. There is so much that I want to do, so much that is waiting to be done. O God, give me the patience that I know I must have. Make me a little better every day until, bit by bit, I am well again. Amen.

Deafness
I used to hear so well and loved what I heard, human voices, music, birds, traffic. Now I'm in a silent world, Lord. People shout at me and grow cross when I don't hear. This embarrasses and hurts me. I pray that I may accept it more. Amen.

Prayer for cheerfulness
Lord, I know that this hospital can never be like home. Yet while I am sick I am thankful for it and for its dedicated staff. Please help me to be cheerful because in that way I will help both myself and others. Amen.

Prayers for healing
Lord, there was an occasion in the Gospel when someone called out: "If it is really your will, make me whole". And you replied: "Of course it is! Be whole!" "I'm crying out now, Lord. I say: If it is your will". Can I take it that it

really is? Can I hope and trust? I really mean it, Jesus. Do you? Amen.

§　§　§

I lie here day in and day out and watch the world go by. And I feel like the cripple at the pool. Somehow I am never the one selected for healing. But I believe you are the true healer, Lord — sometimes through men and women, doctors and others, but sometimes directly. I do not mind how it comes, but Jesus, Son of David, have pity on me. Heal me. Amen.

Prayer for relatives at home
Heavenly Father, watch over my loved ones who remain at home. Keep them safe in body and soul. Take away from them the anxiety and fear they have about me. I leave them all, Lord, in your fatherly care. Amen.

Prayer for other patients
Lord, as we are together, we are each full of pain and distress. Send your healing Spirit to lighten our anxiety, to relieve our suffering, to give us strength to fight this disease, to keep hope and joy alive in our hearts. Lord, you loved the sick in your life-time; show us your love now. Amen.

§　§　§

Lord, I want to pray for all the patients in this hospital. I pray that all who are here sick or

injured, or needing an operation, may learn
more of you while they are here. I pray that
they may be restored to health and strength.
Give them comfort and courage in time of pain.
Give them patience to wait on you, knowing that
all things work together for good to them that
love you. Amen.

Prayer for the staff
O Lord Jesus Christ, I pray for all who work to
make this hospital a place of true healing. I pray
for those I see and meet and for the many others
who work behind the scenes to support them. I
pray that those who treat the body may not
forget the soul and that those who serve the
spiritual may not despise the body; but that they
may all work together for the cure of all sickness
and disease. Amen.

Prayer for a sick child
O Lord Jesus Christ, you came into the world in
the form of a little child. On this earth you
showed your love for children. Bless my/this
child who is sick. Relieve his/her pain; guard
him/her from danger and bring him/her back to
health. Amen.

**Prayer for those who have no one to pray for
them**
Lord, accept my prayers for those who have no
one to pray for them. Wherever and whoever
they are, give them a share of your blessings and

in your love let them know they are not
forgotten. Amen.

Prayers of thanksgiving
O Lord, my God, I cried to you in my troubles
and you heard me. I put my trust in you and
have not been disappointed. You have turned
my sorrow into joy and guided me with your
light. Therefore I praise you with all my heart
and give thanks to your holy name forever.
Amen.

§   §   §

O God, I thank you for the many mercies you
gave me during my stay in hospital. I thank you
for my health and for friendships made. I look
forward to reunion with my family and friends. I
look forward to going back to work and enjoying
the beautiful things your world contains. May I
leave this hospital a kinder and more grateful
person. Amen.

Short Prayers
Lord, I ask you to think of me in my sickness,
because sometimes it is hard to bear.

§   §   §

Lord, help me to keep going.

§   §   §

Lord, if you are willing, take this cup away from me. Nevertheless, let your will be done, not mine.

§ § §

Your Father knows what you need before you ask him. Pray then like this: Our Father . . . etc.

§ § §

Remember the other sick. My misfortunes may be nothing compared to theirs.

§ § §

Remember those who work here giving their lives for the benefit of others and the good people who come round to visit. Thank you, Lord, it is you who helps them do it.

The Rosary

The Rosary is a meditation on the main events of Christ's life and saving work.

The Five Joyful Mysteries
(Monday and Thursday)
1. The Annunciation
2. The Visitation
3. The Birth of Our Lord
4. The Presentation in the Temple

5. The Finding of the Child Jesus in the Temple

The Five Sorrowful Mysteries
(Tuesday and Friday)
  1. The Agony in the Garden
  2. The Scourging at the Pillar
  3. The Crowning with Thorns
  4. The Carrying of the Cross
  5. The Crucifixion and Death of Our Lord

The Five Glorious Mysteries
(Wednesday, Saturday and Sunday)
  1. The Resurrection
  2. The Ascension of Christ into Heaven
  3. The Coming of the Holy Spirit on the Apostles
  4. The Assumption of Our Lady
  5. The Crowning of our Lady as Queen of Heaven

Hail Holy Queen etc.
Let us Pray.
O God, whose only begotten Son, by His life, death and resurrection, has purchased for us the rewards of eternal life; grant, we beseech you, that meditating on these Mysteries of the most holy Rosary of the Blessed Virgin Mary, we may both initiate what they contain and obtain what they promise, through the same Christ our Lord.
                                        Amen

The Way of the Cross

This devotion began in Jerusalem when people prayed at the places associated with the passion and death of Our Lord.

The Way of the Cross puts you in contact with Christ at the supreme moment of His Life. You enter into his suffering and He shares with you the virtues He displayed at that hour — resignation, patience, perseverance, acceptance faith and confidence in the Father. Christ did not come to do away with suffering. He did not come to explain it. He came to fill it with His presence.

> You may begin each station by saying:
> We adore you, O Christ, and we bless you.
> Because by your Holy Cross you have
>   redeemed the world.

and end with,

> — Our Father, Hail Mary, Glory be
> or
> I love you, Jesus, my love above all things.
> I repent with my whole heart of having
>   offended You.
> Never permit me to separate myself from you
>   again,
> Grant that I may always love you and then do
>   with me what you will.

Opening Prayer
Lord Jesus Christ, help me to meditate

prayerfully on your journey to Calvary and on your death and resurrection.

As I pray the Way of the Cross, I do so with a sense of hope, because I know that your Resurrection on Easter Sunday followed your death on Good Friday. Jesus, because you conquered death, I know that death is not the end but rather the beginning of a new life with Christ, free from pain, sorrow and separation.

First Station:
Jesus is condemned to death
Jesus, Pilate condemned you unfairly;
I pray for all who are unfairly condemned;
Help me not to judge others unfairly.

Second Station:
Jesus carries his cross
Jesus, I have a cross to bear — my illness;
I pray for all who have a cross to bear;
Help me to accept my cross patiently and if it cannot be removed, give me the strength to carry it.

Third Station:
Jesus falls the first time
Jesus, you are now so weak that you fall;
I pray for all who are ill;
Help me to get better, if it is Your will.

Fourth Station:
Jesus meets his Mother
Jesus, your mother suffered as she watched

you carry your cross;
I pray for all parents;
help me to appreciate the sacrifices my parents
made (make) for me.

Fifth Station:
Simon of Cyrene helps Jesus to carry his cross
Jesus, Simon helped, though reluctantly;
I pray for all who, through illness,
help you carry your cross;
Help me to see it that way.

Sixth Station:
Veronica wipes the face of Jesus
Jesus, you accepted Veronica's kindness,
gentleness and caring:
I pray for all who care for me;
Help me to accept the assistance and care I
need.

Seventh Station:
Jesus falls the second time
Jesus, you must have been close to despair at
this time.
I pray for all who feel like that.
Help me to have faith in you.

Eighth Station:
Jesus speaks to the women of Jerusalem
Jesus, the women approached you and you
responded angrily;
I pray for all who cannot understand that many
times anger is not meant personally;

Help me, when I am angry, to dissipate it in a healthy way.

Ninth Station:
Jesus falls the third time
Jesus, you must have found the constant effort difficult;
I pray for all who suffer from a long-term illness;
Help me to have trust and confidence in you and so persevere in faith.

Tenth Station:
Jesus is stripped of his garments
Jesus, you were stripped of your garments;
I pray for all who have neither clothing, food nor housing;
Help me to offer my suffering for all those in the world who have neither clothing, food nor housing.

Eleventh Station:
Jesus is nailed to the cross
Jesus, your pain was severe;
I pray for everyone enduring pain of any kind;
Help me to offer my pain for all mankind and particularly for those dear to me whose needs I know. Let the bearing of my pain be my prayer.

Twelfth Station:
Jesus dies on the cross
Jesus, you died on the cross for me and for all;
forgive me all my sins;

31

I pray for all who die today;
Help me and be with me at the hour of my
death for I place all my trust in you.

Thirteenth Station:
Jesus' body is taken down from the cross
Jesus, your body was placed in the arms of your
afflicted Mother;
I pray for all parents who lose a son or daughter
in death;
Help me to remain close to Mary, Mother of the
Church.

Fourteenth Station:
Jesus' body is laid in the tomb
Jesus, your Mother and disciples mourned you;
I pray for all who mourn;
Help me, when grief comes to me,
to know that my loved ones are with You
and help me to maintain my hope of eternal life.

Fifteenth Station:
The Resurrection of Jesus
Jesus, on the third day you rose from the dead;
I pray for all who have died in Christ;
Help me to realise that in order to live with you
I must first learn to die with you.

Sixteenth Station:
The coming of the Holy Spirit
Jesus, you sent the Holy Spirit to be with us
forever;
I pray for everyone in the world;

Help me to be open to the Spirit as Mary and the
Apostles were and lead me, through the Holy Spirit,
to the fullness of your love.

Concluding Prayer
Dying you have destroyed our Death
Rising you restored our life
Lord Jesus come in glory.
            Amen.

Morning Prayers

In the Name of the Father . . . etc.

I thank you Lord, for bringing me safely through the night. You have given me another day to love and serve you.

§ § §

Lord, I offer myself to you this day. Especially I offer the worries, pains and boredom that come my way because I am in hospital. Help me to have perfect trust in you so that nothing may frighten or worry me. I unite myself with your sufferings. May I always live in your love.

§ § §

Bless and protect all families, especially my own loved ones at home. May the light of Your Presence shine out to the world through them.

§ § §

Comfort all who are patients in this hospital. Bring them healing through the dedicated skill of the doctors and nurses. Bless the many others who work behind the scenes to support them.

§ § §

Fill my heart with the Spirit of your love so that I may love you and share my love of you by being thoughtful and considerate to others.

§ § §

Our Father. Hail Mary. Glory be to the Father.

The Memorare

Remember, O most gracious Virgin Mary, that never was it known, that anyone who fled to your protection, implored your aid or sought your intercession, was left unaided. Inspired with this confidence, I fly to you, O Virgin of Virgins, my Mother. To you do I come, before you do I stand, sinful and sorrowful. O Mother of the Word Incarnate, despise not my petitions but graciously hear and answer them. Amen.

Night Prayers

In the Name of the Father . . . etc.

§ § §

Our Father. Hail Mary. Glory be to the Father.

§ § §

At the end of the day, Lord, I thank you for all your love and help. Give me light to see what sins I have committed, and give me the grace to be truly sorry for them.

§ § §

Bless my family at home and all who are dear to me. Reward those who have been kind to me. Comfort those who are in sorrow.

Have mercy on the sick and dying.

§ § §

Grant that what I have suffered today to be of help to someone somewhere.

§ § §

I pray for all those facing operations or various tests and X-rays tomorrow.

§ § §

God, our Father, do not let me be anxious about what might happen tomorrow, for you who care for me today will take care of me tomorrow also and every day of my life.

§ § §

Give me restful sleep and the peace of heart that comes from knowing that our sins are forgiven and that we are always in your loving care. Amen.

Prayers before Confession

Lord, be merciful to me, a sinner! I know I have gone astray. Help me to make a good confession. Amen.

"Come now, let us talk this over",
says God.
"Though your sins are like scarlet,
they shall be as white as snow;
though they are red as crimson,
they shall be like wool."

(Is 1:18)

"The blood of Jesus
purifies us from all sin."

(I Jn 1:76)

Prayer after Confession

"No need to recall the past, no need to think of what was done before". *(Is 43:18)*

Prayers before Holy Communion

"Take this all of you and eat it:
This is My Body which will be given up for
you."

"Take this all of you and drink from it:
This is the cup of My Blood,
the Blood of the new and everlasting covenant.
It will be shed for you and for all
so that sins may be forgiven.
Do this in memory of Me."

"Anyone who eats My Flesh and drinks My
Blood has eternal life, and I will raise him up on
the last day." *(Jn 6:55)*.

Prayer for Help
O my God, help me to make a good
Communion.
Mary, my mother, pray to Jesus for me. Amen.

Act of Sorrow
O my God, I am sorry for my sins. I will try not
to sin again. Forgive me.

Lord, I am not worthy to receive you, but only
say the word and I will be healed.

Act of Faith
O my God, because you have said it, I believe
that I will receive the Sacred Body of Jesus
Christ to eat and His Precious Blood to drink.
My God, I believe this with all my heart.

Act of Love and Desire
O Jesus, I love you. I desire with all my heart to receive you. Give me your Flesh to eat and your Blood to drink. Give me your whole self that I may live for ever with you. Amen.

Prayers after Holy Communion
(Pick the prayers you like best)

Jesus, I believe I have received your Body and Blood in Holy Communion.

§   §   §

Jesus, I adore you.

§   §   §

I thank you for this gift of yourself.

§   §   §

Blessed be Jesus in the most Holy Sacrament of the Altar.

§   §   §

Lord, you have come to me in Holy Communion. With Mary, our Mother, I wish to adore you: I want to thank you and to praise you and above all to love you.

§   §   §

Soul of Christ, make me holy.
Body of Christ, save me.
Blood of Christ, fill me with joy.
Water from the side of Christ, wash me.
Passion of Christ, strengthen me.
O kind Jesus, hear me.
Hide me within Your wounds,
and never let me be parted from You.
Defend me from the wicked enemy.
Call me at the hour of my death
and bid me to come to You
That I may praise You with Your saints
for ever and ever. Amen.

§   §   §

Lord you tell me in the words of your prophet:
Do not be afraid, I have redeemed you,
I have called you by your name, you are mine.
Because you are "precious in my eyes", "I love
you".

Lord, can it be true, "precious in my eyes", "I
love you"? and yet I know it is true. What can I
say? Lord, I am not worthy, but come Lord
Jesus, come.

§   §   §

Now that you have received Holy Communion,
Christ is saying to you:

"Go and take me with you. I don't Myself walk
visibly among people. I can only go where you

41

will take Me; I can only speak when you will
loan me your voice. It is only through your lips
and your eyes that I can show compassion
towards the unfortunate, and patience towards
the ignorant and the weak. It is only through
your hands that I can give help to the needy.
Only through your pity can I show love towards
the unlovable. Only in you and with you can I
walk among people and be seen by them and be
recognised and loved''.

§ § §

Lord, I believe in you: increase my faith.
I trust in you: strengthen my trust:
I love you: let me love you more and more.
I am sorry for my sins: deepen my sorrow.

I worship you as my first beginning.
I long for you as my last end.
I praise you as my constant helper,
and call on you as my loving protector.

§ § §

Jesus said: ''Know that **I am with you always:**
yes, to the end of time''. *(Mt 28:20)*

Prayers for the Dying

When visiting or with a dying person, prayer is very helpful, both for ourselves and the dying. Do not be too shy to pray. It is important to **be simple** *as this is easier for the patient to grasp when weak and failing.*

(1)   Decade of the the Rosary
      Maybe 1st Sorrowful Mystery —
            The Agony in the Garden
   or   1st Glorious Mystery —
            The Resurrection
(2)   Act of Contrition

Jesus, Mary and Joseph, we give you his/her heart and his/her soul.

Jesus, Mary and Joseph, assist him/her now and in his/her last agony.

Jesus, Mary and Joseph, may he/she breathe forth his/her soul in peace with you. Into your hands, O Lord, I/we commend his/her spirit.

Lord Jesus, receive his/her soul.

I wish that where I am they also may be with me, says the Lord Jesus.   *(John 17:24)*

All who believe in the Son, will have eternal life.
                                    (John 6:40)

We have an everlasting home in heaven.
                                    (2 Cor 5:1)

Prayers after death

(1)   Decade of the Rosary
       1st Glorious Mystery — The Resurrection

(2)   Lord, for your faithful people life is changed, not ended.
       When the body of our earthly dwelling lies in death we gain an everlasting dwelling place in heaven.

(3)   Let us pray.
       Now that our brother/sister, (N) has passed from this life, we commend him/her to you, Lord.
       May he/she live in your presence.
       In your mercy and love, forgive whatever sins he/she may have committed through human weakness.

We ask this through Christ our Lord.
Amen.

Selection for Maternity

Introduction

A maternity ward can be a place of worry, sorrow or joy.

You may be worried about a safe delivery, about yourself or about your family at home. You wonder how the others will manage while you are away.

You may be sorrowful because of uncertainty about your baby, because you have lost your baby or because you have to wait a while.

Or you may be joyful, rejoicing in the birth of your child.

In whatever situation you find yourself we hope that you will find a prayer here to suit you. If you do, say it slowly and let God speak to you through your prayer.

Baptism

Now that you have given birth to your child you will soon be having him/her baptised. You will share with him/her your spiritual life and attach him/her to Christ and to the Church. You care for the natural life of your children by feeding them, teaching them and loving them. You must also care for their spiritual life. When you have your children baptised, you take on the responsibility of bringing them up as Catholics and preparing them for the sacraments of Penance, Holy Communion and Confirmation.

You will teach them to pray, to give and to
forgive, to tell the truth and to respect others. It
was at home and from the example of your
parents that you first learned these virtues. One
word at home is better than a thousand words in
the church or in the school or anywhere else.
Generally speaking, good children come from
good homes.

It is very important that you have the right
atmosphere in your home, not over pious, not
lax, but with a healthy respect for religion, and
that you teach your children by the good
example of your daily life.

Prayers

Prayer for a child in the womb
Almighty God, Author of life, I thank you for
the gift of new life.
Bless our child in my womb.
Protect him or her from all harm.
Grant that he or she will be a healthy child.
Grant that he or she will receive the sacrament
of Baptism and grow up in grace to serve You
and the Church.
I make my prayer through Christ our Lord.

Amen.

Prayers for a safe delivery
Lord, the months of waiting are ended and my
time is almost here. Take away all tension and
fear; make me relaxed and unafraid. Strengthen
me for my delivery and give me joy in

remembering that through me you are sending another human person into the world. Amen.

I recall the words of Jesus "A woman in childbirth suffers, because her time has come: but when she has given birth to the child she forgets the suffering in her joy that a child has been born into the world". May any anxiety that I now feel be turned into the joy of a safe delivery. Stay with me, Lord, during my time of waiting and give me the patience I need. Be with me especially in my hour of delivery to strengthen me and give me courage. May my child come to the light of day and be a healthy baby. Protect my baby from all danger, from all injury and from all harm. Amen.

Thanksgiving after delivery
Lord, thank you for bringing me and my baby safely through everything. Bless my baby. Keep him/her safe in all the dangers of childhood. Bring him/her safely through the hazards of youth and grant that he/she may grow up to be a fully mature person. Amen.

§ § §

Help me always to be a good mother to the baby you have now given to me; to be kind, loving and understanding. Help me to teach him/her to love God and love his/her neighbour as Jesus himself came on earth to teach us. Bless me now; You have given me the wonderful experience of motherhood. Help me to be always true to my responsibility as a mother and never to fail in the trust you have now given to me. Help me to make my home a place where there is a Christian atmosphere of prayer, joy and a healthy respect for religion among all the members of the family. Help us to remember you when trouble and sorrow come our way. Let us never forget that you are always present in our home. Guide us in our decisions and help us over all our difficulties. Amen.

Dedication of a child to Mary
Mary, Mother of God, take this child under your tender care. Watch over him/her always. Grant that his/her journey through this world may lead to eternal life. We ask this through Christ our Lord. Amen.

Prayer of Parents
Heavenly Father, you have given to us the opportunity and responsibility of bringing new life into the world. Bless us in our joys and sorrows. Deepen our love for one another and for our children. We are the first bearers of your word and your love to them. Remind us often that we have no riches or training to give them without you. Amen.

Prayer for a sick baby
Lord, I pray to you for my baby who is sick. If it is your will, grant that he/she may be brought to perfect health. Amen.

Prayer for a handicapped baby
Lord, we know that Your Ways are not our
ways. This is a heavy cross we have to bear.
Give us the grace to bear it. We know that this
child is made in the likeness of God and will be
with God for all eternity. Help us to accept
whatever lies in store for this child of Yours and
ours. We know that out of this sorrow some joy
must come. Amen.

**Prayer of a mother in danger of
losing her baby**
Lord, I am afraid I might lose my baby. I don't
know what to say to you. Please help me. Amen.

Prayer of a mother who has lost her baby
Father in heaven, only you know the sorrow that
weighs me down at this moment. I ask for your
support in my sorrow and distress. Surround me
with your love. Help me to face the future with
courage and hope. I pray for healing in my heart
and in my spirit. Remind me that my baby isn't
really lost but is now enjoying the happiness of
heaven "where all tears are wiped away and
where there is no more mourning or sadness".
Help me to go back home without any bitterness
or resentment to take up again my tasks in life.
Grant that this suffering may deepen and
strengthen my love for you and my love for
those around me. Amen.

§ § §

Lord, our hearts are heavy with sorrow. We ask you to comfort us in our sorrow. Give us the courage to face the future with good hope. Teach us to use this pain for all who suffer so that we may share in your work of turning sorrow into joy; through Christ our Lord. Amen.

§　§　§

"See that you never despise any of these little ones for I tell you that their angels in heaven are continually in the presence of my Father in Heaven".

(Mt 18:10)

Prayers of an unmarried mother
Dear Lord, thank you for bringing my baby safely to birth. You did not fail me when I felt alone and afraid. Thank you for the wonderful experience of being a mother.

§　§　§

Bless my baby, Lord, and protect it always. Be with me now as I worry about the future. Help me to do what is best for the baby, for I know that this is what you want me to do, and that it will bring me happiness also. Give me wisdom, courage and peace of mind.

§　§　§

Lord, surround me with your love and care. Help me to have faith in myself because you have faith in me. Open my heart to bring joy and friendship into the lives of others. Amen.

A Nurse's Prayer

O God, teach me to receive the sick in your
name.
For the glory of Your Holy Name, give success
to my efforts.
It is Your work that I do: without you I cannot
succeed.
Grant that the sick you have placed in my care
may be abundantly blessed, and not one of them
be lost because of any neglect on my part.

Help me to overcome every temporal weakness,
and
strengthen in me whatever may enable me to
bring joy to the lives of those I serve.

Give me grace, for the sake of your sick ones
and of those whose lives will be influenced by
them.

Amen.

A Doctor's Prayer

Lord, Thou Great Physician, I pray to
you, since every good and perfect gift
must come from you.
    I pray:
Give skill to my hand, clear vision to
my mind, kindness and sympathy to my heart.
Give me singleness of purpose, strength to

lift at least a part of the burden of my
suffering fellows, and a true realisation
of the rare privilege that is mine. Take
from my heart all guile and worldliness,
that with the simple faith of a child I
may rely on you.

Amen.

Prayer of One who Works with the Sick

Lord Jesus Christ,
I ask you to be with me as
I serve those closest to you.

Help me
to look on them with love,
to listen attentively to their needs,
to speak kind words to them and

above all,
to appreciate that in serving them
I am serving you.

Amen.

Scripture Quotes for Various Occasions

In time of fear or anxiety
Do not be afraid, for I am with you;
Stop being anxious and watchful, for I am your
God.
I give you strength, I bring you help,
I uphold you with my victorious right hand.

(Is 41:10)

Do not be afraid, for I have redeemed you;
I have called you by your name, you are mine.
Should you pass through the sea, I will be with
you;
or through rivers, they will not swallow you up.
Should you walk through fire, you will not be
scorched
and the flames will not burn you.
For I am . . . . your God,
          your Saviour.

(Is 43:1b-3)

Do not be afraid; only have faith.

(Mk 5:36)

God Himself has said: I will not fail you or
desert you, and so we can say with confidence:
with the Lord to help me, I fear nothing:
what can man do to me.

(Heb 13:5-6)

In time of loneliness
The Lord is my Shepherd,
there is nothing I shall want. *(Repeat)*

(Ps 22:1)

In time of sadness
And sadness came over him,
and great distress. Then he said to them
"My soul is sorrowful to the point of
death" . . .
And going on a little further, he fell on
his face and prayed. "My Father", he said,
'if it is possible, let this cup pass me by.
Nevertheless, let it be as you, not I, would have
it'.

(Mt 26:37-39)

In time of mental or physical suffering
It makes me happy to suffer for you as I am
suffering now, and in my own body to do all
that I can to make up all that has still to be
undergone by Christ for the sake of His Body,
the Church.

(Col 1:24)

**Here, in his letter to the Colossians, St Paul is
telling us that illness is not to be seen as a
time of helplessness or uselessness. Rather,
those who accept suffering are sharing in some
mysterious way in the redemptive work of
Christ for all people.**

. . . I was given a thorn in the flesh, . . .
I have pleaded with the Lord three times for it

54

to leave me, but he has said: "My grace is
enough for you; my power is at its best in
weakness".

(II Cor 12:7-8)

Think of what Christ suffered in this life, and
then arm yourselves with the same resolution
that he had: anyone who in this life has bodily
suffering has broken with sin, because for the
rest of his life on earth he is not ruled by human
passions but only by the will of God.

(I Peter 4:1)

In time of anger
Daughters of Jerusalem, do not weep for me;
weep rather for yourselves and for your children.
For the days will surely come when people will
say — 'Happy are those who are barren, the
wombs that never bore, the breasts that have
never sucked'! Then they will begin to say to
the mountains, "Fall on us!" to the hills,
"Cover us!" For if men use the green wood like
this, what will happen when it is dry?'

(Lk 23:28-30)

Feeling deserted by God
My God, my God, why have you forsaken me?
You are far from my plea and the cry of my
distress.
O my God, I call by day and you give no reply;
I call by night and I find no peace.

Do not leave me alone in my distress; come
closer, there is none else to help.

O Lord, do not leave me alone, my strength,
make haste to help me.

My soul shall live for Him . . .
declare his faithfulness to peoples yet unborn.

(Ps 2:1-2, 12, 20, 32)

Does a woman forget her baby at the breast,
or fail to cherish the son of her womb?
Yet even if these forget,
I will never forget you
See, I have branded you on the palms of my
hands.

(Is 49:15—16)

In time of grief or mourning
Jesus wept; and the Jews said, 'See how much
he loved him!'

(Jn 11:37)

We want you to be quite certain about those
who have died, to make sure that you do not
grieve about them, like the other people who
have no hope. We believe that Jesus died and
rose again, and that it will be the same for those
who have died in Jesus: God will bring them
with him.
With such thoughts as these you should comfort
one another.

(I Thess 4:13-14, 18)

Longing for God
God, you are my God, I am seeking you,

my soul is thirsting for you,
. . .I long to gaze on you in the Sanctuary,
and to see your power and glory.

(Ps 63:1-2)